STEP-BY-STEP WEDDING PLANNER

Activinotes

DAILY JOURNALS, PLANNERS, NOTEBOOKS AND OTHER BLANK BOOKS

_____

BRIDE'S NAME

_____

GROOM'S NAME

_____

WEDDING DATE

_____

WEDDING PLANNER

"THE MOST SUCCESSFUL
EVENT IS THE ONE THAT
ACHIEVES YOUR GOALS
AND EXCEEDS YOUR
EXPECTATION"

WEDDING PLANNER

TOP PRIORITY

IMPORTANT

SHOULD DO

GETTING AROUND TO

RECEPTION PLANNER

GENERAL INFORMATION

Groom's Name::

Bride's Name:

Event Date: _____   # of Guest: _____

Event Location: _____
_____

How you like your Disc Jockey attired?
_____ Formal   _____ Semi Formal   _____ Casual

What type of food service are you having?
_____ Seated Dinner   _____ Dinner Buffet

PROGRAM & MUSIC EVENTS

Ceremony Start Time: _____ AM/PM   Are we going to provide the msic? Yes / No

Ceremony Location: _____

Reception Start Time: _____ AM/PM

Dinner/Cocktail Music:
_____Contemporary Jazz   _____Love Songs   _____Classic

TRADITIONAL EVENTS

Time:
Announcing of the Wedding Party: Yes/No

Flower Girl: _____   Ring Bearer: _____
Flower Girl: _____   Bible Bearer: _____
Flower Girl: _____   Groomsman: _____
Bridesmaid: _____   Groomsman: _____
Bridesmaid: _____   Groomsman: _____
Bridesmaid: _____   Groomsman: _____
Maid/Matron of Honor: _____   Bestman: _____

Announcing of the Bride & Groom: _____

WEDDING BUDGET PLANNER

	MAX	ESTIMATE	ACTUAL	PAYEE	DEPOSIT	BALANCE
WE'RE GETTING MARRIED STATIONERY						
GETTING THERE						
IN LOCATION						
CEREMONY						
LEGAL						
RECEPTION						

GUEST LIST WORKSHEET

LIST OF NAMES	INVITE SENT	TABLE NUMBER	THANK YOU SENT

CHECKLIST

- ☐ _____
- ☐ _____
- ☐ _____
- ☐ _____
- ☐ _____
- ☐ _____
- ☐ _____
- ☐ _____
- ☐ _____
- ☐ _____
- ☐ _____
- ☐ _____

- ☐ _____
- ☐ _____
- ☐ _____
- ☐ _____
- ☐ _____
- ☐ _____
- ☐ _____
- ☐ _____
- ☐ _____
- ☐ _____
- ☐ _____
- ☐ _____

WEDDING PLANNER

TOP PRIORITY

IMPORTANT

SHOULD DO

GETTING AROUND TO

Reception Planner

GENERAL INFORMATION

Groom's Name::

Bride's Name:

Event Date: _____   # of Guest: _____

Event Location: _____
_____

How you like your Disc Jockey attired?
_____ Formal   _____ Semi Formal   _____ Casual

What type of food service are you having?
_____ Seated Dinner   _____ Dinner Buffet

PROGRAM & MUSIC EVENTS

Ceremony Start Time: _____ AM/PM   Are we going to provide the msic? Yes / No

Ceremony Location: _____

Reception Start Time: _____ AM/PM

Dinner/Cocktail Music:
_____Contemporary Jazz   _____Love Songs   _____Classic

TRADITIONAL EVENTS

Time:
Announcing of the Wedding Party: Yes/No

Flower Girl: _____   Ring Bearer: _____
Flower Girl: _____   Bible Bearer: _____
Flower Girl: _____   Groomsman: _____
Bridesmaid: _____   Groomsman: _____
Bridesmaid: _____   Groomsman: _____
Bridesmaid: _____   Groomsman: _____
Maid/Matron of Honor: _____   Bestman: _____

Announcing of the Bride & Groom: _____

WEDDING BUDGET PLANNER

	MAX	ESTIMATE	ACTUAL	PAYEE	DEPOSIT	BALANCE
WE'RE GETTING MARRIED STATIONERY						
GETTING THERE						
IN LOCATION						
CEREMONY						
LEGAL						
RECEPTION						

GUEST LIST WORKSHEET

LIST OF NAMES	INVITE SENT	TABLE NUMBER	THANK YOU SENT

CHECKLIST

- [ ] _____
- [ ] _____
- [ ] _____
- [ ] _____
- [ ] _____
- [ ] _____
- [ ] _____
- [ ] _____
- [ ] _____
- [ ] _____
- [ ] _____
- [ ] _____

- [ ] _____
- [ ] _____
- [ ] _____
- [ ] _____
- [ ] _____
- [ ] _____
- [ ] _____
- [ ] _____
- [ ] _____
- [ ] _____
- [ ] _____
- [ ] _____

WEDDING PLANNER

TOP PRIORITY

IMPORTANT

SHOULD DO

GETTING AROUND TO

Reception Planner

GENERAL INFORMATION

Groom's Name::

Bride's Name:

Event Date: _____   # of Guest: _____

Event Location: _____
_____

How you like your Disc Jockey attired?
_____ Formal   _____ Semi Formal   _____ Casual

What type of food service are you having?
_____ Seated Dinner   _____ Dinner Buffet

PROGRAM & MUSIC EVENTS

Ceremony Start Time: _____ AM/PM   Are we going to provide the msic? Yes / No

Ceremony Location: _____

Reception Start Time: _____ AM/PM

Dinner/Cocktail Music:
_____Contemporary Jazz   _____Love Songs   _____Classic

TRADITIONAL EVENTS

Time:
Announcing of the Wedding Party: Yes/No

Flower Girl: _____   Ring Bearer: _____
Flower Girl: _____   Bible Bearer: _____
Flower Girl: _____   Groomsman: _____
Bridesmaid: _____   Groomsman: _____
Bridesmaid: _____   Groomsman: _____
Bridesmaid: _____   Groomsman: _____
Maid/Matron of Honor: _____   Bestman: _____

Announcing of the Bride & Groom: _____

WEDDING BUDGET PLANNER

	MAX	ESTIMATE	ACTUAL	PAYEE	DEPOSIT	BALANCE
WE'RE GETTING MARRIED STATIONERY						
GETTING THERE						
IN LOCATION						
CEREMONY						
LEGAL						
RECEPTION						

GUEST LIST WORKSHEET

LIST OF NAMES	INVITE SENT	TABLE NUMBER	THANK YOU SENT

CHECKLIST

- ☐ _____
- ☐ _____
- ☐ _____
- ☐ _____
- ☐ _____
- ☐ _____
- ☐ _____
- ☐ _____
- ☐ _____
- ☐ _____
- ☐ _____

- ☐ _____
- ☐ _____
- ☐ _____
- ☐ _____
- ☐ _____
- ☐ _____
- ☐ _____
- ☐ _____
- ☐ _____
- ☐ _____
- ☐ _____

WEDDING PLANNER

TOP PRIORITY

IMPORTANT

SHOULD DO

GETTING AROUND TO

RECEPTION PLANNER

GENERAL INFORMATION

Groom's Name::

Bride's Name:

Event Date: _____   # of Guest: _____

Event Location: _____
_____

How you like your Disc Jockey attired?
_____ Formal   _____ Semi Formal   _____ Casual

What type of food service are you having?
_____ Seated Dinner   _____ Dinner Buffet

PROGRAM & MUSIC EVENTS

Ceremony Start Time: _____ AM/PM   Are we going to provide the msic? Yes / No

Ceremony Location: _____

Reception Start Time: _____ AM/PM

Dinner/Cocktail Music:
_____Contemporary Jazz   _____Love Songs   _____Classic

TRADITIONAL EVENTS

Time:
Announcing of the Wedding Party: Yes/No

Flower Girl: _____   Ring Bearer: _____
Flower Girl: _____   Bible Bearer: _____
Flower Girl: _____   Groomsman: _____
Bridesmaid: _____   Groomsman: _____
Bridesmaid: _____   Groomsman: _____
Bridesmaid: _____   Groomsman: _____
Maid/Matron of Honor: _____   Bestman: _____

Announcing of the Bride & Groom: _____

WEDDING BUDGET PLANNER

	MAX	ESTIMATE	ACTUAL	PAYEE	DEPOSIT	BALANCE
WE'RE GETTING MARRIED STATIONERY						
GETTING THERE						
IN LOCATION						
CEREMONY						
LEGAL						
RECEPTION						

GUEST LIST WORKSHEET

LIST OF NAMES	INVITE SENT	TABLE NUMBER	THANK YOU SENT

CHECKLIST

☐ _____   ☐ _____

☐ _____   ☐ _____

☐ _____   ☐ _____

☐ _____   ☐ _____

☐ _____   ☐ _____

☐ _____   ☐ _____

☐ _____   ☐ _____

☐ _____   ☐ _____

☐ _____   ☐ _____

☐ _____   ☐ _____

☐ _____   ☐ _____

☐ _____   ☐ _____

WEDDING PLANNER

TOP PRIORITY

IMPORTANT

SHOULD DO

GETTING AROUND TO

RECEPTION PLANNER

GENERAL INFORMATION

Groom's Name::

Bride's Name:

Event Date: _____   # of Guest: _____

Event Location: _____
_____

How you like your Disc Jockey attired?
_____ Formal   _____ Semi Formal   _____ Casual

What type of food service are you having?
_____ Seated Dinner   _____ Dinner Buffet

PROGRAM & MUSIC EVENTS

Ceremony Start Time: _____ AM/PM   Are we going to provide the msic? Yes / No

Ceremony Location: _____

Reception Start Time: _____ AM/PM

Dinner/Cocktail Music:
_____Contemporary Jazz   _____Love Songs   _____Classic

TRADITIONAL EVENTS

Time:
Announcing of the Wedding Party: Yes/No

Flower Girl: _____	Ring Bearer: _____
Flower Girl: _____	Bible Bearer: _____
Flower Girl: _____	Groomsman: _____
Bridesmaid: _____	Groomsman: _____
Bridesmaid: _____	Groomsman: _____
Bridesmaid: _____	Groomsman: _____
Maid/Matron of Honor: _____	Bestman: _____

Announcing of the Bride & Groom: _____

WEDDING BUDGET PLANNER

	MAX	ESTIMATE	ACTUAL	PAYEE	DEPOSIT	BALANCE
WE'RE GETTING MARRIED STATIONERY						
GETTING THERE						
IN LOCATION						
CEREMONY						
LEGAL						
RECEPTION						

GUEST LIST WORKSHEET

LIST OF NAMES	INVITE SENT	TABLE NUMBER	THANK YOU SENT

CHECKLIST

- ☐ _____
- ☐ _____
- ☐ _____
- ☐ _____
- ☐ _____
- ☐ _____
- ☐ _____
- ☐ _____
- ☐ _____
- ☐ _____
- ☐ _____
- ☐ _____

- ☐ _____
- ☐ _____
- ☐ _____
- ☐ _____
- ☐ _____
- ☐ _____
- ☐ _____
- ☐ _____
- ☐ _____
- ☐ _____
- ☐ _____
- ☐ _____

WEDDING PLANNER

TOP PRIORITY

IMPORTANT

SHOULD DO

GETTING AROUND TO

RECEPTION PLANNER

GENERAL INFORMATION

Groom's Name::

Bride's Name:

Event Date: _____   # of Guest: _____

Event Location: _____
_____

How you like your Disc Jockey attired?
_____ Formal   _____ Semi Formal   _____ Casual

What type of food service are you having?
_____ Seated Dinner   _____ Dinner Buffet

PROGRAM & MUSIC EVENTS

Ceremony Start Time: _____ AM/PM   Are we going to provide the msic? Yes / No

Ceremony Location: _____

Reception Start Time: _____ AM/PM

Dinner/Cocktail Music:
_____Contemporary Jazz   _____Love Songs   _____Classic

TRADITIONAL EVENTS

Time:
Announcing of the Wedding Party: Yes/No

Flower Girl: _____	Ring Bearer: _____
Flower Girl: _____	Bible Bearer: _____
Flower Girl: _____	Groomsman: _____
Bridesmaid: _____	Groomsman: _____
Bridesmaid: _____	Groomsman: _____
Bridesmaid: _____	Groomsman: _____
Maid/Matron of Honor: _____	Bestman: _____

Announcing of the Bride & Groom: _____

WEDDING BUDGET PLANNER

	MAX	ESTIMATE	ACTUAL	PAYEE	DEPOSIT	BALANCE
WE'RE GETTING MARRIED STATIONERY						
GETTING THERE						
IN LOCATION						
CEREMONY						
LEGAL						
RECEPTION						

GUEST LIST WORKSHEET

LIST OF NAMES	INVITE SENT	TABLE NUMBER	THANK YOU SENT

CHECKLIST

- ☐ _____
- ☐ _____
- ☐ _____
- ☐ _____
- ☐ _____
- ☐ _____
- ☐ _____
- ☐ _____
- ☐ _____
- ☐ _____
- ☐ _____
- ☐ _____

- ☐ _____
- ☐ _____
- ☐ _____
- ☐ _____
- ☐ _____
- ☐ _____
- ☐ _____
- ☐ _____
- ☐ _____
- ☐ _____
- ☐ _____
- ☐ _____

WEDDING PLANNER

TOP PRIORITY

IMPORTANT

SHOULD DO

GETTING AROUND TO

RECEPTION PLANNER

GENERAL INFORMATION

Groom's Name::

Bride's Name:

Event Date: _____   # of Guest: _____

Event Location: _____
_____

How you like your Disc Jockey attired?
_____ Formal   _____ Semi Formal   _____ Casual

What type of food service are you having?
_____ Seated Dinner   _____ Dinner Buffet

PROGRAM & MUSIC EVENTS

Ceremony Start Time: _____ AM/PM   Are we going to provide the msic? Yes / No

Ceremony Location: _____

Reception Start Time: _____ AM/PM

Dinner/Cocktail Music:
_____Contemporary Jazz   _____Love Songs   _____Classic

TRADITIONAL EVENTS

Time:
Announcing of the Wedding Party: Yes/No

Flower Girl: _____	Ring Bearer: _____
Flower Girl: _____	Bible Bearer: _____
Flower Girl: _____	Groomsman: _____
Bridesmaid: _____	Groomsman: _____
Bridesmaid: _____	Groomsman: _____
Bridesmaid: _____	Groomsman: _____
Maid/Matron of Honor: _____	Bestman: _____

Announcing of the Bride & Groom: _____

WEDDING BUDGET PLANNER

	MAX	ESTIMATE	ACTUAL	PAYEE	DEPOSIT	BALANCE
WE'RE GETTING MARRIED STATIONERY						
GETTING THERE						
IN LOCATION						
CEREMONY						
LEGAL						
RECEPTION						

GUEST LIST WORKSHEET

LIST OF NAMES	INVITE SENT	TABLE NUMBER	THANK YOU SENT

CHECKLIST

- [ ] _____
- [ ] _____
- [ ] _____
- [ ] _____
- [ ] _____
- [ ] _____
- [ ] _____
- [ ] _____
- [ ] _____
- [ ] _____
- [ ] _____

- [ ] _____
- [ ] _____
- [ ] _____
- [ ] _____
- [ ] _____
- [ ] _____
- [ ] _____
- [ ] _____
- [ ] _____
- [ ] _____
- [ ] _____

WEDDING PLANNER

TOP PRIORITY

IMPORTANT

SHOULD DO

GETTING AROUND TO

RECEPTION PLANNER

GENERAL INFORMATION

Groom's Name::

Bride's Name:

Event Date: _____   # of Guest: _____

Event Location: _____
_____

How you like your Disc Jockey attired?
_____ Formal   _____ Semi Formal   _____ Casual

What type of food service are you having?
_____ Seated Dinner   _____ Dinner Buffet

PROGRAM & MUSIC EVENTS

Ceremony Start Time: _____ AM/PM   Are we going to provide the msic? Yes / No

Ceremony Location: _____

Reception Start Time: _____ AM/PM

Dinner/Cocktail Music:
_____ Contemporary Jazz   _____ Love Songs   _____ Classic

TRADITIONAL EVENTS

Time:
Announcing of the Wedding Party: Yes/No

Flower Girl: _____	Ring Bearer: _____
Flower Girl: _____	Bible Bearer: _____
Flower Girl: _____	Groomsman: _____
Bridesmaid: _____	Groomsman: _____
Bridesmaid: _____	Groomsman: _____
Bridesmaid: _____	Groomsman: _____
Maid/Matron of Honor: _____	Bestman: _____

Announcing of the Bride & Groom: _____

WEDDING BUDGET PLANNER

	MAX	ESTIMATE	ACTUAL	PAYEE	DEPOSIT	BALANCE
WE'RE GETTING MARRIED STATIONERY						
GETTING THERE						
IN LOCATION						
CEREMONY						
LEGAL						
RECEPTION						

GUEST LIST WORKSHEET

LIST OF NAMES	INVITE SENT	TABLE NUMBER	THANK YOU SENT

CHECKLIST

- ☐ _____
- ☐ _____
- ☐ _____
- ☐ _____
- ☐ _____
- ☐ _____
- ☐ _____
- ☐ _____
- ☐ _____
- ☐ _____
- ☐ _____
- ☐ _____

- ☐ _____
- ☐ _____
- ☐ _____
- ☐ _____
- ☐ _____
- ☐ _____
- ☐ _____
- ☐ _____
- ☐ _____
- ☐ _____
- ☐ _____
- ☐ _____

WEDDING PLANNER

TOP PRIORITY

IMPORTANT

SHOULD DO

GETTING AROUND TO

RECEPTION PLANNER

GENERAL INFORMATION

Groom's Name::

Bride's Name:

Event Date: _____   # of Guest: _____

Event Location: _____
_____

How you like your Disc Jockey attired?

_____ Formal   _____ Semi Formal   _____ Casual

What type of food service are you having?

_____ Seated Dinner   _____ Dinner Buffet

PROGRAM & MUSIC EVENTS

Ceremony Start Time: _____ AM/PM   Are we going to provide the msic? Yes / No

Ceremony Location: _____

Reception Start Time: _____ AM/PM

Dinner/Cocktail Music:

_____Contemporary Jazz   _____Love Songs   _____Classic

TRADITIONAL EVENTS

Time:
Announcing of the Wedding Party: Yes/No

Flower Girl: _____	Ring Bearer: _____
Flower Girl: _____	Bible Bearer: _____
Flower Girl: _____	Groomsman: _____
Bridesmaid: _____	Groomsman: _____
Bridesmaid: _____	Groomsman: _____
Bridesmaid: _____	Groomsman: _____
Maid/Matron of Honor: _____	Bestman: _____

Announcing of the Bride & Groom: _____

WEDDING BUDGET PLANNER

	MAX	ESTIMATE	ACTUAL	PAYEE	DEPOSIT	BALANCE
WE'RE GETTING MARRIED STATIONERY						
GETTING THERE						
IN LOCATION						
CEREMONY						
LEGAL						
RECEPTION						

GUEST LIST WORKSHEET

LIST OF NAMES	INVITE SENT	TABLE NUMBER	THANK YOU SENT

CHECKLIST

☐ _____

☐ _____

☐ _____

☐ _____

☐ _____

☐ _____

☐ _____

☐ _____

☐ _____

☐ _____

☐ _____

☐ _____

☐ _____

☐ _____

☐ _____

☐ _____

☐ _____

☐ _____

☐ _____

☐ _____

☐ _____

☐ _____

WEDDING PLANNER

TOP PRIORITY

IMPORTANT

SHOULD DO

GETTING AROUND TO

Reception Planner

GENERAL INFORMATION

Groom's Name::

Bride's Name:

Event Date: _____   # of Guest: _____

Event Location: _____
_____

How you like your Disc Jockey attired?
_____ Formal   _____ Semi Formal   _____ Casual

What type of food service are you having?
_____ Seated Dinner   _____ Dinner Buffet

PROGRAM & MUSIC EVENTS

Ceremony Start Time: _____ AM/PM   Are we going to provide the msic? Yes / No

Ceremony Location: _____

Reception Start Time: _____ AM/PM

Dinner/Cocktail Music:
_____Contemporary Jazz   _____Love Songs   _____Classic

TRADITIONAL EVENTS

Time:
Announcing of the Wedding Party: Yes/No

Flower Girl: _____	Ring Bearer: _____
Flower Girl: _____	Bible Bearer: _____
Flower Girl: _____	Groomsman: _____
Bridesmaid: _____	Groomsman: _____
Bridesmaid: _____	Groomsman: _____
Bridesmaid: _____	Groomsman: _____
Maid/Matron of Honor: _____	Bestman: _____

Announcing of the Bride & Groom: _____

WEDDING BUDGET PLANNER

	MAX	ESTIMATE	ACTUAL	PAYEE	DEPOSIT	BALANCE
WE'RE GETTING MARRIED STATIONERY						
GETTING THERE						
IN LOCATION						
CEREMONY						
LEGAL						
RECEPTION						

GUEST LIST WORKSHEET

LIST OF NAMES	INVITE SENT	TABLE NUMBER	THANK YOU SENT

CHECKLIST

☐ _____   ☐ _____

☐ _____   ☐ _____

☐ _____   ☐ _____

☐ _____   ☐ _____

☐ _____   ☐ _____

☐ _____   ☐ _____

☐ _____   ☐ _____

☐ _____   ☐ _____

☐ _____   ☐ _____

☐ _____   ☐ _____

☐ _____   ☐ _____

☐ _____   ☐ _____

WEDDING PLANNER

TOP PRIORITY

IMPORTANT

SHOULD DO

GETTING AROUND TO

Reception Planner

GENERAL INFORMATION

Groom's Name::

Bride's Name:

Event Date: _____   # of Guest: _____

Event Location: _____
_____

How you like your Disc Jockey attired?

_____ Formal   _____ Semi Formal   _____ Casual

What type of food service are you having?

_____ Seated Dinner   _____ Dinner Buffet

PROGRAM & MUSIC EVENTS

Ceremony Start Time: _____ AM/PM   Are we going to provide the msic? Yes / No

Ceremony Location: _____

Reception Start Time: _____ AM/PM

Dinner/Cocktail Music:

_____Contemporary Jazz   _____Love Songs   _____Classic

TRADITIONAL EVENTS

Time:
Announcing of the Wedding Party: Yes/No

Flower Girl: _____   Ring Bearer: _____
Flower Girl: _____   Bible Bearer: _____
Flower Girl: _____   Groomsman: _____
Bridesmaid: _____   Groomsman: _____
Bridesmaid: _____   Groomsman: _____
Bridesmaid: _____   Groomsman: _____
Maid/Matron of Honor: _____   Bestman: _____

Announcing of the Bride & Groom: _____

WEDDING BUDGET PLANNER

	MAX	ESTIMATE	ACTUAL	PAYEE	DEPOSIT	BALANCE
WE'RE GETTING MARRIED STATIONERY						
GETTING THERE						
IN LOCATION						
CEREMONY						
LEGAL						
RECEPTION						

GUEST LIST WORKSHEET

LIST OF NAMES	INVITE SENT	TABLE NUMBER	THANK YOU SENT

CHECKLIST

☐ _____   ☐ _____

☐ _____   ☐ _____

☐ _____   ☐ _____

☐ _____   ☐ _____

☐ _____   ☐ _____

☐ _____   ☐ _____

☐ _____   ☐ _____

☐ _____   ☐ _____

☐ _____   ☐ _____

☐ _____   ☐ _____

☐ _____   ☐ _____

☐ _____   ☐ _____

WEDDING PLANNER

TOP PRIORITY

IMPORTANT

SHOULD DO

GETTING AROUND TO

Reception Planner

GENERAL INFORMATION

Groom's Name::

Bride's Name:

Event Date: _____   # of Guest: _____

Event Location: _____
_____

How you like your Disc Jockey attired?
_____ Formal   _____ Semi Formal   _____ Casual

What type of food service are you having?
_____ Seated Dinner   _____ Dinner Buffet

PROGRAM & MUSIC EVENTS

Ceremony Start Time: _____ AM/PM   Are we going to provide the msic? Yes / No

Ceremony Location: _____

Reception Start Time: _____ AM/PM

Dinner/Cocktail Music:
_____Contemporary Jazz   _____Love Songs   _____Classic

TRADITIONAL EVENTS

Time:
Announcing of the Wedding Party: Yes/No

Flower Girl: _____   Ring Bearer: _____

Flower Girl: _____   Bible Bearer: _____

Flower Girl: _____   Groomsman: _____

Bridesmaid: _____   Groomsman: _____

Bridesmaid: _____   Groomsman: _____

Bridesmaid: _____   Groomsman: _____

Maid/Matron of Honor: _____   Bestman: _____

Announcing of the Bride & Groom: _____

WEDDING BUDGET PLANNER

	MAX	ESTIMATE	ACTUAL	PAYEE	DEPOSIT	BALANCE
WE'RE GETTING MARRIED STATIONERY						
GETTING THERE						
IN LOCATION						
CEREMONY						
LEGAL						
RECEPTION						

GUEST LIST WORKSHEET

LIST OF NAMES	INVITE SENT	TABLE NUMBER	THANK YOU SENT

CHECKLIST

- ☐ _____
- ☐ _____
- ☐ _____
- ☐ _____
- ☐ _____
- ☐ _____
- ☐ _____
- ☐ _____
- ☐ _____
- ☐ _____
- ☐ _____
- ☐ _____

- ☐ _____
- ☐ _____
- ☐ _____
- ☐ _____
- ☐ _____
- ☐ _____
- ☐ _____
- ☐ _____
- ☐ _____
- ☐ _____
- ☐ _____
- ☐ _____

WEDDING PLANNER

TOP PRIORITY

IMPORTANT

SHOULD DO

GETTING AROUND TO

RECEPTION PLANNER

GENERAL INFORMATION

Groom's Name::

Bride's Name:

Event Date: _____   # of Guest: _____

Event Location: _____
_____

How you like your Disc Jockey attired?

_____ Formal   _____ Semi Formal   _____ Casual

What type of food service are you having?

_____ Seated Dinner   _____ Dinner Buffet

PROGRAM & MUSIC EVENTS

Ceremony Start Time: _____ AM/PM   Are we going to provide the msic? Yes / No

Ceremony Location: _____

Reception Start Time: _____ AM/PM

Dinner/Cocktail Music:

_____Contemporary Jazz   _____Love Songs   _____Classic

TRADITIONAL EVENTS

Time:

Announcing of the Wedding Party: Yes/No

Flower Girl: _____   Ring Bearer: _____
Flower Girl: _____   Bible Bearer: _____
Flower Girl: _____   Groomsman: _____
Bridesmaid: _____   Groomsman: _____
Bridesmaid: _____   Groomsman: _____
Bridesmaid: _____   Groomsman: _____
Maid/Matron of Honor: _____   Bestman: _____

Announcing of the Bride & Groom: _____

WEDDING BUDGET PLANNER

	MAX	ESTIMATE	ACTUAL	PAYEE	DEPOSIT	BALANCE
WE'RE GETTING MARRIED STATIONERY						
GETTING THERE						
IN LOCATION						
CEREMONY						
LEGAL						
RECEPTION						

GUEST LIST WORKSHEET

LIST OF NAMES	INVITE SENT	TABLE NUMBER	THANK YOU SENT

CHECKLIST

☐ _____   ☐ _____

☐ _____   ☐ _____

☐ _____   ☐ _____

☐ _____   ☐ _____

☐ _____   ☐ _____

☐ _____   ☐ _____

☐ _____   ☐ _____

☐ _____   ☐ _____

☐ _____   ☐ _____

☐ _____   ☐ _____

☐ _____   ☐ _____

WEDDING PLANNER

TOP PRIORITY

IMPORTANT

SHOULD DO

GETTING AROUND TO

Reception Planner

GENERAL INFORMATION

Groom's Name::

Bride's Name:

Event Date: _____   # of Guest: _____

Event Location: _____
_____

How you like your Disc Jockey attired?
_____ Formal   _____ Semi Formal   _____ Casual

What type of food service are you having?
_____ Seated Dinner   _____ Dinner Buffet

PROGRAM & MUSIC EVENTS

Ceremony Start Time: _____ AM/PM   Are we going to provide the msic? Yes / No

Ceremony Location: _____

Reception Start Time: _____ AM/PM

Dinner/Cocktail Music:
_____Contemporary Jazz   _____Love Songs   _____Classic

TRADITIONAL EVENTS

Time:
Announcing of the Wedding Party: Yes/No

Flower Girl: _____   Ring Bearer: _____

Flower Girl: _____   Bible Bearer: _____

Flower Girl: _____   Groomsman: _____

Bridesmaid: _____   Groomsman: _____

Bridesmaid: _____   Groomsman: _____

Bridesmaid: _____   Groomsman: _____

Maid/Matron of Honor: _____   Bestman: _____

Announcing of the Bride & Groom: _____

WEDDING BUDGET PLANNER

	MAX	ESTIMATE	ACTUAL	PAYEE	DEPOSIT	BALANCE
WE'RE GETTING MARRIED Stationery						
GETTING THERE						
IN LOCATION						
CEREMONY						
LEGAL						
RECEPTION						

GUEST LIST WORKSHEET

LIST OF NAMES	INVITE SENT	TABLE NUMBER	THANK YOU SENT

CHECKLIST

☐ _____   ☐ _____

☐ _____   ☐ _____

☐ _____   ☐ _____

☐ _____   ☐ _____

☐ _____   ☐ _____

☐ _____   ☐ _____

☐ _____   ☐ _____

☐ _____   ☐ _____

☐ _____   ☐ _____

☐ _____   ☐ _____

☐ _____   ☐ _____

☐ _____   ☐ _____

WEDDING PLANNER

TOP PRIORITY

IMPORTANT

SHOULD DO

GETTING AROUND TO

Reception Planner

GENERAL INFORMATION

Groom's Name::

Bride's Name:

Event Date: _____   # of Guest: _____

Event Location: _____

_____

How you like your Disc Jockey attired?

_____ Formal   _____ Semi Formal   _____ Casual

What type of food service are you having?

_____ Seated Dinner   _____ Dinner Buffet

PROGRAM & MUSIC EVENTS

Ceremony Start Time: _____ AM/PM   Are we going to provide the msic? Yes / No

Ceremony Location: _____

Reception Start Time: _____ AM/PM

Dinner/Cocktail Music:

_____Contemporary Jazz   _____Love Songs   _____Classic

TRADITIONAL EVENTS

Time:

Announcing of the Wedding Party: Yes/No

Flower Girl: _____   Ring Bearer: _____

Flower Girl: _____   Bible Bearer: _____

Flower Girl: _____   Groomsman: _____

Bridesmaid: _____   Groomsman: _____

Bridesmaid: _____   Groomsman: _____

Bridesmaid: _____   Groomsman: _____

Maid/Matron of Honor: _____   Bestman: _____

Announcing of the Bride & Groom: _____

WEDDING BUDGET PLANNER

	MAX	ESTIMATE	ACTUAL	PAYEE	DEPOSIT	BALANCE
WE'RE GETTING MARRIED STATIONERY						
GETTING THERE						
IN LOCATION						
CEREMONY						
LEGAL						
RECEPTION						

GUEST LIST WORKSHEET

LIST OF NAMES	INVITE SENT	TABLE NUMBER	THANK YOU SENT

CHECKLIST

☐ _____   ☐ _____

☐ _____   ☐ _____

☐ _____   ☐ _____

☐ _____   ☐ _____

☐ _____   ☐ _____

☐ _____   ☐ _____

☐ _____   ☐ _____

☐ _____   ☐ _____

☐ _____   ☐ _____

☐ _____   ☐ _____

☐ _____   ☐ _____

☐ _____   ☐ _____

WEDDING PLANNER

TOP PRIORITY

IMPORTANT

SHOULD DO

GETTING AROUND TO

RECEPTION PLANNER

GENERAL INFORMATION

Groom's Name::

Bride's Name:

Event Date: _____   # of Guest: _____

Event Location: _____
_____

How you like your Disc Jockey attired?
_____ Formal   _____ Semi Formal   _____ Casual

What type of food service are you having?
_____ Seated Dinner   _____ Dinner Buffet

PROGRAM & MUSIC EVENTS

Ceremony Start Time: _____ AM/PM   Are we going to provide the msic? Yes / No

Ceremony Location: _____

Reception Start Time: _____ AM/PM

Dinner/Cocktail Music:
_____Contemporary Jazz   _____Love Songs   _____Classic

TRADITIONAL EVENTS

Time:
Announcing of the Wedding Party: Yes/No

Flower Girl: _____	Ring Bearer: _____
Flower Girl: _____	Bible Bearer: _____
Flower Girl: _____	Groomsman: _____
Bridesmaid: _____	Groomsman: _____
Bridesmaid: _____	Groomsman: _____
Bridesmaid: _____	Groomsman: _____
Maid/Matron of Honor: _____	Bestman: _____

Announcing of the Bride & Groom: _____

WEDDING BUDGET PLANNER

	MAX	ESTIMATE	ACTUAL	PAYEE	DEPOSIT	BALANCE
WE'RE GETTING MARRIED STATIONERY						
GETTING THERE						
IN LOCATION						
CEREMONY						
LEGAL						
RECEPTION						

GUEST LIST WORKSHEET

LIST OF NAMES	INVITE SENT	TABLE NUMBER	THANK YOU SENT

CHECKLIST

☐ _____

☐ _____

☐ _____

☐ _____

☐ _____

☐ _____

☐ _____

☐ _____

☐ _____

☐ _____

☐ _____

☐ _____

☐ _____

☐ _____

☐ _____

☐ _____

☐ _____

☐ _____

☐ _____

☐ _____

☐ _____

☐ _____

WEDDING PLANNER

TOP PRIORITY

IMPORTANT

SHOULD DO

GETTING AROUND TO

Reception Planner

GENERAL INFORMATION

Groom's Name::

Bride's Name:

Event Date: _____   # of Guest: _____

Event Location: _____
_____

How you like your Disc Jockey attired?

_____ Formal   _____ Semi Formal   _____ Casual

What type of food service are you having?

_____ Seated Dinner   _____ Dinner Buffet

PROGRAM & MUSIC EVENTS

Ceremony Start Time: _____ AM/PM   Are we going to provide the msic? Yes / No

Ceremony Location: _____

Reception Start Time: _____ AM/PM

Dinner/Cocktail Music:

_____Contemporary Jazz   _____Love Songs   _____Classic

TRADITIONAL EVENTS

Time:
Announcing of the Wedding Party: Yes/No

Flower Girl: _____   Ring Bearer: _____
Flower Girl: _____   Bible Bearer: _____
Flower Girl: _____   Groomsman: _____
Bridesmaid: _____   Groomsman: _____
Bridesmaid: _____   Groomsman: _____
Bridesmaid: _____   Groomsman: _____
Maid/Matron of Honor: _____   Bestman: _____

Announcing of the Bride & Groom: _____

WEDDING BUDGET PLANNER

	MAX	ESTIMATE	ACTUAL	PAYEE	DEPOSIT	BALANCE
WE'RE GETTING MARRIED STATIONERY						
GETTING THERE						
IN LOCATION						
CEREMONY						
LEGAL						
RECEPTION						

GUEST LIST WORKSHEET

LIST OF NAMES	INVITE SENT	TABLE NUMBER	THANK YOU SENT

CHECKLIST

☐ _____

☐ _____

☐ _____

☐ _____

☐ _____

☐ _____

☐ _____

☐ _____

☐ _____

☐ _____

☐ _____

☐ _____

☐ _____

☐ _____

☐ _____

☐ _____

☐ _____

☐ _____

☐ _____

☐ _____

☐ _____

☐ _____

WEDDING PLANNER

TOP PRIORITY

IMPORTANT

SHOULD DO

GETTING AROUND TO

RECEPTION PLANNER

GENERAL INFORMATION

Groom's Name::

Bride's Name:

Event Date: _____   # of Guest: _____

Event Location: _____
_____

How you like your Disc Jockey attired?
_____ Formal   _____ Semi Formal   _____ Casual

What type of food service are you having?
_____ Seated Dinner   _____ Dinner Buffet

PROGRAM & MUSIC EVENTS

Ceremony Start Time: _____ AM/PM   Are we going to provide the msic? Yes / No

Ceremony Location: _____

Reception Start Time: _____ AM/PM

Dinner/Cocktail Music:
_____Contemporary Jazz   _____Love Songs   _____Classic

TRADITIONAL EVENTS

Time:
Announcing of the Wedding Party: Yes/No

Flower Girl: _____	Ring Bearer: _____
Flower Girl: _____	Bible Bearer: _____
Flower Girl: _____	Groomsman: _____
Bridesmaid: _____	Groomsman: _____
Bridesmaid: _____	Groomsman: _____
Bridesmaid: _____	Groomsman: _____
Maid/Matron of Honor: _____	Bestman: _____

Announcing of the Bride & Groom: _____

WEDDING BUDGET PLANNER

	MAX	ESTIMATE	ACTUAL	PAYEE	DEPOSIT	BALANCE
WE'RE GETTING MARRIED STATIONERY						
GETTING THERE						
IN LOCATION						
CEREMONY						
LEGAL						
RECEPTION						

GUEST LIST WORKSHEET

LIST OF NAMES	INVITE SENT	TABLE NUMBER	THANK YOU SENT

CHECKLIST

- [ ] _____
- [ ] _____
- [ ] _____
- [ ] _____
- [ ] _____
- [ ] _____
- [ ] _____
- [ ] _____
- [ ] _____
- [ ] _____
- [ ] _____
- [ ] _____

- [ ] _____
- [ ] _____
- [ ] _____
- [ ] _____
- [ ] _____
- [ ] _____
- [ ] _____
- [ ] _____
- [ ] _____
- [ ] _____
- [ ] _____
- [ ] _____

WEDDING PLANNER

TOP PRIORITY

IMPORTANT

SHOULD DO

GETTING AROUND TO

RECEPTION PLANNER

GENERAL INFORMATION

Groom's Name::

Bride's Name:

Event Date: _____   # of Guest: _____

Event Location: _____
_____

How you like your Disc Jockey attired?

_____ Formal   _____ Semi Formal   _____ Casual

What type of food service are you having?

_____ Seated Dinner   _____ Dinner Buffet

PROGRAM & MUSIC EVENTS

Ceremony Start Time: _____ AM/PM   Are we going to provide the msic? Yes / No

Ceremony Location: _____

Reception Start Time: _____ AM/PM

Dinner/Cocktail Music:

_____Contemporary Jazz   _____Love Songs   _____Classic

TRADITIONAL EVENTS

Time:

Announcing of the Wedding Party: Yes/No

Flower Girl: _____   Ring Bearer: _____

Flower Girl: _____   Bible Bearer: _____

Flower Girl: _____   Groomsman: _____

Bridesmaid: _____   Groomsman: _____

Bridesmaid: _____   Groomsman: _____

Bridesmaid: _____   Groomsman: _____

Maid/Matron of Honor: _____   Bestman: _____

Announcing of the Bride & Groom: _____

WEDDING BUDGET PLANNER

	MAX	ESTIMATE	ACTUAL	PAYEE	DEPOSIT	BALANCE
WE'RE GETTING MARRIED STATIONERY						
GETTING THERE						
IN LOCATION						
CEREMONY						
LEGAL						
RECEPTION						

GUEST LIST WORKSHEET

LIST OF NAMES	INVITE SENT	TABLE NUMBER	THANK YOU SENT

CHECKLIST

☐ _____   ☐ _____

☐ _____   ☐ _____

☐ _____   ☐ _____

☐ _____   ☐ _____

☐ _____   ☐ _____

☐ _____   ☐ _____

☐ _____   ☐ _____

☐ _____   ☐ _____

☐ _____   ☐ _____

☐ _____   ☐ _____

☐ _____   ☐ _____

☐ _____   ☐ _____

WEDDING PLANNER

TOP PRIORITY

IMPORTANT

SHOULD DO

GETTING AROUND TO

Reception Planner

GENERAL INFORMATION

Groom's Name::

Bride's Name:

Event Date: _____   # of Guest: _____

Event Location: _____
_____

How you like your Disc Jockey attired?
_____ Formal   _____ Semi Formal   _____ Casual

What type of food service are you having?
_____ Seated Dinner   _____ Dinner Buffet

PROGRAM & MUSIC EVENTS

Ceremony Start Time: _____ AM/PM   Are we going to provide the msic? Yes / No

Ceremony Location: _____

Reception Start Time: _____ AM/PM

Dinner/Cocktail Music:
_____Contemporary Jazz   _____Love Songs   _____Classic

TRADITIONAL EVENTS

Time:
Announcing of the Wedding Party: Yes/No

Flower Girl: _____   Ring Bearer: _____
Flower Girl: _____   Bible Bearer: _____
Flower Girl: _____   Groomsman: _____
Bridesmaid: _____   Groomsman: _____
Bridesmaid: _____   Groomsman: _____
Bridesmaid: _____   Groomsman: _____
Maid/Matron of Honor: _____   Bestman: _____

Announcing of the Bride & Groom: _____

WEDDING BUDGET PLANNER

	MAX	ESTIMATE	ACTUAL	PAYEE	DEPOSIT	BALANCE
WE'RE GETTING MARRIED STATIONERY						
GETTING THERE						
IN LOCATION						
CEREMONY						
LEGAL						
RECEPTION						

GUEST LIST WORKSHEET

LIST OF NAMES	INVITE SENT	TABLE NUMBER	THANK YOU SENT

CHECKLIST

☐ ＿＿＿＿＿＿＿＿＿＿＿＿＿＿

☐ ＿＿＿＿＿＿＿＿＿＿＿＿＿＿

☐ ＿＿＿＿＿＿＿＿＿＿＿＿＿＿

☐ ＿＿＿＿＿＿＿＿＿＿＿＿＿＿

☐ ＿＿＿＿＿＿＿＿＿＿＿＿＿＿

☐ ＿＿＿＿＿＿＿＿＿＿＿＿＿＿

☐ ＿＿＿＿＿＿＿＿＿＿＿＿＿＿

☐ ＿＿＿＿＿＿＿＿＿＿＿＿＿＿

☐ ＿＿＿＿＿＿＿＿＿＿＿＿＿＿

☐ ＿＿＿＿＿＿＿＿＿＿＿＿＿＿

☐ ＿＿＿＿＿＿＿＿＿＿＿＿＿＿

☐ ＿＿＿＿＿＿＿＿＿＿＿＿＿＿

☐ ＿＿＿＿＿＿＿＿＿＿＿＿＿＿

☐ ＿＿＿＿＿＿＿＿＿＿＿＿＿＿

☐ ＿＿＿＿＿＿＿＿＿＿＿＿＿＿

☐ ＿＿＿＿＿＿＿＿＿＿＿＿＿＿

☐ ＿＿＿＿＿＿＿＿＿＿＿＿＿＿

☐ ＿＿＿＿＿＿＿＿＿＿＿＿＿＿

☐ ＿＿＿＿＿＿＿＿＿＿＿＿＿＿

☐ ＿＿＿＿＿＿＿＿＿＿＿＿＿＿

☐ ＿＿＿＿＿＿＿＿＿＿＿＿＿＿

☐ ＿＿＿＿＿＿＿＿＿＿＿＿＿＿

CHECKLIST

☐ _____   ☐ _____

☐ _____   ☐ _____

☐ _____   ☐ _____

☐ _____   ☐ _____

☐ _____   ☐ _____

☐ _____   ☐ _____

☐ _____   ☐ _____

☐ _____   ☐ _____

☐ _____   ☐ _____

☐ _____   ☐ _____

☐ _____   ☐ _____

☐ _____   ☐ _____

www.ingramcontent.com/pod-product-compliance
Lightning Source LLC
Chambersburg PA
CBHW081336090426
42737CB00017B/3173